Blended Nutrition

50 Recipes For Your Blender

And Your Health

by

John L. James

www.BlendedNutritionBook.com

"Today, more than 95% of all chronic disease is caused by food choice, toxic food ingredients, nutritional deficiencies and lack of physical exercise."

– Mike Adams, author, investigative journalist, educator

Dedication

To my family - my mother Muriel, sisters Susan and Diane, and my brother James - for always being there for me especially when I deserved it the least but needed it the most.

Contents

Why Blending

For years fitness gurus have been teaching the benefits of juicing. You may have heard of "The Godfather of fitness" Jack LaLanne. For many of those years Jack has been talking about Juicing as a way to get the nutrients we need from our fruits and vegetables.

Here is a quote directly from his website:
"Smart choices can help lead to a healthier you. One with more energy and vigor. While a healthy diet consists of many things one of them is the daily intake of fruits and vegetables. It is recommended we eat 5-9 servings daily to help keep our bodies healthy. You think there's not enough time in the day to eat what's recommended well juicing might just be the perfect solution to the common problem. Juicing is a quick and easy way to get all the goodness fruits and vegetables have to offer. Deliver a tremendous amount of vitamins, minerals, nutrients and enzymes without having to digest and breakdown the food first."

You can also learn about juicing from "The Father of Juicing", Jay Kordich, Best Selling New York Times

Author of The Juiceman's Power of Juicing. Jay, and his wife Linda, are still very strong, vibrant and vital! While pushing 90 years old, Jay has been teaching the power and benefits of juicing since 1948.

Traditional juicing is a great way to get many of the nutrients that we are missing in today's fast paced diets. However, traditional juicing is missing one thing that is very important to our health and the quality and longevity of our lives. Fiber!

We suggest blended nutrition so you can retain the fiber that is naturally found in whole foods. Some of the benefits to be had from including sufficient fiber in your food plan include:

1. Fiber helps you feel full longer resulting in consuming fewer calories.

2. Fiber will help maintain healthy cholesterol levels - higher HDL and lower LDL.

3. Fiber increase contributes to a healthier blood pressure level.

4. Fiber slows the absorption of sugars helping to avoid diabetes.

5. Fiber blocks the absorption of some of the calories we eat causing weight loss.

6. High fiber supports strong bones and a healthier brain into our advancing years.

7. Fiber acts like a broom in the digestive track sweeping away harmful toxins that will otherwise build up and be reabsorbed until being eliminated from our blood stream and bowel.

The Surgeon General, National Institutes of Health, American Heat Association, and American Diabetes Association all recommend consuming 20 - 35 grams of fiber daily to maintain your health. The average American consumes 8-10 grams at best. It is suggested that a ratio of 65%-75% insoluble fiber to 25%-35% soluble is ideal. You can safely ingest up to 60 grams of fiber. Supplementing your whole food diet may be helpful to reach your goal intake. There are great supplements available. Check out ww.blendednutritionbook.com/fiber.

At first additional fiber intake may cause gas or bloating. If this occurs, you can try increasing your fiber more gradually. Add 5 grams for a few days, then, add 5 more grams until the desired total grams is reached. It is strongly recommended that you increase your clean water consumption - up to half you weight in ounces daily. Stepping up your exercise routine may also help you get relief.

If you just stick with it you will be rewarded with improved wellness and a longer, happier, healthier life.
Now, who doesn't want this?!!!

Choosing The Right Blender

With the hundreds of blenders out there to choose from this can seem a little overwhelming. What company makes the best blender, the color I like, shape, horsepower, capacity, model, and warranty. How do I choose and by what criteria?

The first thing I look at when I look at any product is the company itself. More specifically, will they be there after the purchase has been made? I have the Vitamix 5200 and every time I have called or emailed the company I have talked to prompt, friendly, caring people that were most concerned with me getting the help I needed, unlike other call centers that care more about how much time they are on the phone, or better said, how fast they can get me off the phone. (Sorry for my rant on what I think is wrong with customer service – kind of.)

I have looked at and researched some of the top blenders on the market over the years. While there are a few notables, that I will mention later, the one blender that I keep coming back to every time, and recommend almost exclusively for the average person is the Vita-Mix 5200.

To order and get Free Shipping, go to http://www.BlendedNutritionBook.com/Vitamix.

Some of the reasons why I recommend the Vita-Mix 5200 are as follows.

- New Eastman Tritan™ copolyester 64 oz. container is as durable as polycarbonate, features improved sound damping and is chemical resistant. Comes with ergonomic soft-grip handle.

- New Swedish-built 2 peak HP motor, custom designed for Vita-Mix, runs substantially cooler with energy savings and improved performance.

- Feedback-type variable speed control provides consistent power regardless of load. Speed ranges from 11 m.p.h. to 240 m.p.h., wider than any standard blender. The Vita-Mix blades spin so fast that they will actually heat up your food for you allowing you to make some amazing hot drinks and soups.

- Unique stainless steel hammermill and cutting "wet" blades process whole foods like no other appliance to deliver up to 3 times the nutrition.

- New soft-touch switches and dial backed by new designer label.

- Patented, spill-proof vented lid with removable lid plug lets you measure and add ingredients safely while Vita-Mix is running.
- Patented tamper for extreme processing power helps when preparing foods such as nut butters and frozen treats.
- Quick and easy clean-up. Just add a few drops of dish soap, some warm water and run for 30 seconds on high. Done!
- A No Risk 30 day in home trial and an incredible 7 Year Warranty that is expandable to 10 Years.

Again, to order and get Free Shipping, go to http://www.BlendedNutritionBook.com/Vitamix

Montel William's My HealthMaster features include:

While the Vitamix may be the Cadillac of blenders they are a bit pricey. A great runner up is the HealthMaster that Montel Williams had created as an inexpensive yet comparable in quality blender. At a little more than half of the price of the Vitamix, it is a great starting point.

You can get it at http://www.BlendedNutritionBook.com/HealthMaster

- Retains the Vitamins, Minerals, Antioxidants, and Phyto-Nutrients
- Centrifugal Friction Cooks Food Naturally
- Extra Large 70 oz. Pitcher with 6 Stainless Steel Blades
- One Blade for Both Wet & Dry Blending
- Fairly comparable to Vitamix and almost half the price

You can get it at
http://www.BlendedNutritionBook.com/HealthMaster

Blendtec Home The Professional's Choice 1560-Watt Total Blender features include:

If for some reason you do not like the above mentioned blenders, do not fret. Blendtec has a great line of high quality blenders that will fit most families needs.

You can Read more here…
http://www.BlendedNutritionBook.com/Blendtecpro

- Commercial-quality 1,560-watt countertop blender with 3 HP direct-drive motor

- Preprogrammed blending cycles; digital touchpad controls; auto shutoff
- 2-prong stainless-steel blade spins at up to 29,000 rpm; ice-crushing guarantee
- 2-quart square blending jar; secure-fitting lid; user guide and recipes included
- Measures 7 by 8 by 15.5 inches; 3-year motor-base warranty; 1-year jar warranty; lifetime coupling-and-blade warranty

You can get it here…
http://www.BlendedNutritionBook.com/Blendtecpro

Drinks and Smoothies

"Never work before breakfast; if you have to work before breakfast, eat your breakfast first." ~Josh Billings

Start Your Day Right!

We have all heard that breakfast is the most important meal of the day but most people do not know why this is. One of the biggest reasons is because a proper healthy breakfast will actually increase your metabolism causing you to burn more calories throughout the day. Burning more calories is the key to loosing more weight faster.

Important Note: Remember to always start your blender on the lowest speed, turn the blender on and then increase the speed.

Berry Power Smoothie

1 to 2 oranges, fresh squeezed
(filtered or bottled water can be used)

1 inch wedge of pineapple
10 to 12 strawberries (frozen organic is fine)
1 cup blueberries (frozen organic is fine)
1 cup broccoli
1 cup kale or spinach
1 serving of your favorite whey protein

1. Place all ingredients into the blender and secure the lid. Be sure to start by putting the water in first.
2. Turn blender on and increase the speed to 10, then flip to switch to high speed.
3. Blend for 1 to 2 minutes, 2 to 3 minutes if using frozen berries. You can add more orange juice or water until desired consistency is reached.

This is my first thing in the morning energy boost. Makes approximately 2 to 3 16 oz. servings. It is great to take with you in a thermos for mid morning or afternoon power boost. It is also heart healthy and vegetarian.

Banana Apple Oatmeal Smoothie

1 cup of water (filtered or bottled is best)
¼ cup low fat vanilla or plain yogurt
½ peeled banana
2 tablespoons uncooked steel cut oats
½ medium apple
¼ cup cranberries (dried or frozen)
1/8 teaspoon ground cinnamon

4. Place all ingredients into the blender and secure the lid. Be sure to start by putting the water in first.
5. Turn blender on and increase the speed to 10, then flip to switch to high speed.
6. Blend for 45 to 60 seconds or until desired consistency is reached.

Not only is the smoothie only 155 calories per 1 cup serving, it is also heart healthy and diabetic friendly. *Vitamix*

Emerald Smoothie

2 cups fresh, ripe pineapple (or 2 in. thick slice)
1 stalk celery (7 in. stalk cut in half)
1 cup gently packed spinach leaves
4 ounces low fat vanilla yogurt (or vanilla soymilk)
2 cups ice cubes
(Optional sweetener if pineapple is tart)

1. Place all ingredients into the blender and secure the lid.
2. Turn blender on and increase the speed to 10, then flip to switch to high speed.
3. Blend for 45 to 60 seconds or until desired consistency is reached.

Best if served immediately. The emerald smoothie has 79 calories per 1 cup serving, and it is also heart healthy and diabetic friendly. *Vitamix*

Going Green Smoothie

1 cup grapes (green or red will work but red grapes may change color slightly)
1/2 cup pineapple
2 cups fresh spinach
½ ripe peeled banana
½ cup of water (filtered or bottled)
1 cup ice cubes

1. Place all ingredients into the blender and secure the lid. Be sure to start by putting the water in first.
2. Turn blender on and increase the speed to 10, then flip to switch to high speed.
3. Blend for 45 to 60 seconds or until desired consistency is reached.

This going green smoothie is only 60 calories per 1 cup serving, it is also heart healthy and diabetic friendly. *Vitamix*

Montel's Green Smoothie

4 cups of water (filtered or bottled is best)
2 peeled banana
3 peeled, quartered oranges
1 head romaine lettuce

1. Place all ingredients into the blender and secure the lid. Be sure to start by putting the water in first.

2. Turn blender on and increase the speed to 10, then flip to switch to high speed.
3. Blend for 45 to 60 seconds or until desired consistency is reached.

Montel's green smoothie only 78 calories per 1/4 of the recipe, it is also heart healthy and diabetic friendly. *Montel Williams*

Kat James' Beauty Detox Elixir

1 ½ cups of water (filtered or bottled is best) or aloe juice
1/3 cup fresh parsley
1 ¾ in. wedge of red cabbage
½ cup dark fresh greens (mustard greens, kale, collards, or dandelion)
1 in. piece of fresh ginger
½ lemon (scrubbed and unpeeled)
½ small beet
Pinch of cayenne pepper or ¼ in. of jalapeno Pepper
Sweetener to taste (agave or stevia)
1 cup ice cubes

1. Place all ingredients into the blender and secure the lid. Be sure to start by putting the water in first.
2. Turn blender on and increase the speed to 10, then flip to switch to high speed.
3. Blend for 45 to 60 seconds or until desired consistency is reached.

Kat James' beauty detox elixir is heart healthy, diabetic friendly, low fat, low sodium, low cholesterol, gluten-free, vegetarian, vegan, and raw. *Kat James*

Before A Workout Smoothie

2 to 3 raw egg whites (since you are using raw egg whites make sure you use pasteurized eggs)
1 peeled banana
1 inch wedge of pineapple
1 tablespoon local raw honey (or agave syrup to taste)
1 teaspoon of coconut extract (or 1 tablespoon raw shredded coconut)

1. Place all ingredients into the blender and secure the lid.
2. Turn blender on and increase to high speed.
3. Blend for 1 to 2 minutes or until desired consistency is reached.

Again, since you are using the egg whites raw, you want to use the regular pasteurized egg whites in the dairy case of your local supermarket. You can also adjust the amount of ice cubes used to make the smoothie thicker or thinner. This pre workout drink is also heart healthy, low fat and raw. *Magic Bullet*

Strawberry Powerhouse Smoothie

1 serving of your favorite protein powder
½ cup strawberries (about 4 to 8)
4 ice cubes
8 ounces ice cold water (you can also use almond milk as a great alternative)

1. Place all ingredients into the blender and secure the lid. Be sure to start by putting the water in first.
2. Turn blender on and increase to high speed.
3. Blend only until ice is ground up.

For a little variety you can substitute you favorite fruit for the strawberries. This is a heart healthy, low fat meal replacement when you find yourself without time for a proper meal. *Magic Bullet*

Banana Cocoa Smoothie

1 to 2 cups almond milk (you can use plain or chocolate if you like)
2 tablespoons cacao nibs
2 frozen medium bananas
4 to 6 ice cubes
¼ cup raw walnuts (optional)

1. Place all ingredients into the blender and secure the lid. Be sure to start by putting the milk in first.

2. Turn blender on and increase to high speed.

3. Blend only until ice is ground up.

For a little variety you can substitute 6 to 10 strawberries for the bananas. This is heart healthy, low fat, and full of protein, vitamins, fiber and, if you use the walnuts, omega-3 fatty acids. *Raw Energy*

Green "Go-Go" Shake

2 medium pealed oranges (you can also use tangerines, or tangelos)
2 cups frozen raspberries
¼ cup raw cashews
¼ cup water (filtered or bottled is best)
1 tablespoon raw, unrefined coconut oil
2 teaspoons Siberian ginseng root power
1 tablespoon spirulina powder

1. Place all ingredients into the blender and secure the lid. Be sure to start by putting the milk in first.

2. Turn blender on and increase to high speed.

3. Blend 60 to 90 seconds or until desired consistency is reached.

This makes a great breakfast when you have a particularly challenging day ahead of you. This is heart healthy, low fat, and full of protein, vitamins, and fiber. *Raw Energy*

Tangerine Dream Smoothie

2 medium pealed oranges (you can also use tangerines, or tangelos)
2 cup almond milk (you can also use walnut milk
1 tablespoon raw, unrefined coconut oil

1. Place all ingredients into the blender and secure the lid. Be sure to start by putting the milk in first.
2. Turn blender on and increase to high speed.
3. Blend 30 to 60 seconds or until desired consistency is reached.

If you like it smoothie style you can add a few ice cubes and blend only until crushed. This is heart healthy, low fat, and full of vitamin C, and fiber.
Raw Energy

Berry Blast Shake

1 ½ cups iced green tea
1 scoop or serving of your favorite vanilla milk protein powder
3 tablespoons low fat plain yogurt
1 serving greens powder (you can get this at most health stores)
3 tablespoons steel cut oats
½ cup frozen mixed berries (blueberries, strawberries, cherries, and raspberries)

1. Place all ingredients into the blender and secure the lid. Be sure to start by putting the green tea in first.
2. Turn blender on and increase to high speed.
3. Blend about 1 to 2 minutes. Only blend long enough to get to the consistency you want. Over blending will only warm the drink.

This is a great shake that is a full meal replacement and has 6 g. of blood sugar stabilizing fiber. This shake has 259 calories and is heart healthy, low fat, low cholesterol, and vegetarian. *Metabolism Advantage*

Apple and Grains Shake

1 ½ cups water
1 scoop or serving of your favorite vanilla milk protein powder
3 tablespoons low fat plain yogurt
1 serving greens powder (you can get this at most health stores)
4 tablespoons steel cut oats
4 tablespoons ground flaxseed
3 tablespoons mixed nuts
1 apple, quartered
Ground cinnamon to taste (optional)

1. Place all ingredients except nuts, apple, and cinnamon into the blender and secure the lid. Be sure to start by putting the water in first.
2. Turn blender on and increase to high speed.
3. Blend about 1 minute. Add the nuts, apple, and cinnamon and blend for about 1 more minute. For a cold shake you can add 4 or 5 ice cubes.

This great meal replacement tastes like applesauce and has 42g. protein and 21g. of fiber. This shake has 516 calories and is heart healthy, low fat, low cholesterol, and vegetarian. *Metabolism Advantage*

Chocolate Nut Shake

1 ½ cups water
1 scoop or serving of your favorite chocolate milk protein powder
3 tablespoons low fat plain yogurt
1 serving greens powder (you can get this at most health stores)
3 tablespoons ground flaxseed
3 tablespoons mixed nuts
1 tablespoon natural peanut butter

1. Place all ingredients except nuts, and peanut butter into the blender and secure the lid. Be sure to start by putting the water in first.
2. Turn blender on and increase to high speed.

3. Blend about 1 minute. Add the nuts, apple, and cinnamon and blend for about 1 more minute. For a cold shake you can add 4 or 5 ice cubes.

Another great meal replacement and has 42g. of protein and 12g. of fiber. This shake has 415 calories and is heart healthy, low cholesterol, and vegetarian. *Metabolism Advantage*

Soups and Sauces

"Our food should be our medicine and our medicine should be our food." – *Hippocrates*

Here are some great tasting recipes that really show you that, while your blender is still great at mixing those drinks, it can do so much more.

Tomato Pasta Sauce

½ cup Vegetable broth or water (filtered or bottled is best)
1 tablespoon olive oil
½ cup chopped yellow or red onion
2 peeled garlic cloves
2 cans (14 oz.) chopped tomatoes, drained
2 tablespoons tomato paste
¼ cup sun dried tomatoes
¼ cup chopped fresh basil

1. Saute onion and garlic in olive oil for 3 minutes
2. Place all ingredients except for half of the sun dried tomatoes and fresh basil into the blender and secure the lid.

3. Turn blender on and increase the speed to 10, then flip to switch to high speed.
4. Blend for 4 to 5 minutes or until the sauce is hot.
5. Remove lid and add the sun dried tomatoes and basil that you kept out earlier. Replace lid.
6. Blend for an additional 20 seconds and serve.

The best part of this sauce is that it is only 44 calories per ½ cup serving, it is also heart healthy, gluten free, vegetarian, and diabetic friendly.
Vitamix

Sweet Potato Soup

1 1/2 cups of water (filtered or bottled is best)
1 vegetable bouillon cube
1 halved baked sweet potato
1 quartered tomato
½ large apple
1 medium carrot
2 tablespoons tomato paste

1. Place all ingredients into the blender and secure the lid. Be sure to start by putting the water in first.
2. Turn blender on and increase the speed to 10, then flip to switch to high speed.
3. Blend for 5 to 6 minutes or until hot.

This is a heart healthy way to eat at only 89 calories per 1 cup serving, it is also gluten free, vegetarian, low cholesterol, and diabetic friendly. *Vitamix*

Butternut Squash Apple Soup

1 ¾ cups chicken broth
1 butternut squash (about 2 lbs.), peeled and cubed
1 medium onion, chopped
2 cups applesauce
½ teaspoon ground ginger
Salt to taste
1 cup low fat sour cream

1. Cook butternut squash until tender (about 3-5 hours).
2. Place all ingredients except for salt and half of the sour cream into the blender and secure the lid. You may only want to blend about half of the mixture at a time.
3. Turn blender on and increase to high speed for 3-5 minutes or until desired temperature is reached.
4. Pour soup into bowls.
5. Add a dollop of sour cream in the center of for garnish and enjoy.

If you substitute non-chicken chicken broth you can keep this a vegetarian meal.

This is not only a great tasting dish with only about 140 calories per serving (makes 8 servings), it is also heart healthy, and gluten free. *Blendtec*

Taco Soup

2 1/2 cups of low sodium chicken stock
1 tablespoon taco seasoning mix
1 tablespoon canned kidney beans
3 tablespoons canned corn
1 halved celery stalk
1 halved tomato (roma or your favorite will do)
1 medium carrot
1 halved onion (green, red, or yellow will work)
¼ cup low fat shredded cheddar cheese
2 cups taco chips
Salt and pepper to taste

1. Place all ingredients into the blender and secure the lid. Be sure to start by putting the chicken stock in first.
2. Turn blender on and increase the speed to 10, then flip to switch to high speed.
3. Blend for 3 to 4 minutes or until hot.
4. Reduce speed to 2 and add taco chips.
5. blend for only 10 to 12 seconds and serve.

This delicious soup is 159 calories per 1 cup serving, it is also low cholesterol, and heart healthy. *Vitamix*

Spicy Green Tomato

1 pint grape tomatoes
6 stalks celery
4 carrots
Handful of spinach
1/3 bunch cilantro
Handful of arugula
2 cloves garlic
1 jalapeno pepper
2 lemons, peeled
1 tablespoon olive oil
1 tablespoon raw honey
Celtic sea salt & freshly ground pepper to taste
½ cup water

1. Place all ingredients into the blender and secure the lid. Be sure to start by putting the water in first.
2. Turn blender on and increase the speed to 10, then flip the switch to high speed.
3. Blend for 1 to 2 minutes adding water to desired consistency. To serve warm as soup blend 5 to 6 minutes.

This is a healthy homemade substitute for V8 juice and a great glass of live nutrition for very few calories per 8oz serving. It is also gluten free, vegetarian, low cholesterol, and diabetic friendly.

Creamy Avocado Soup

1 quart fresh tomatoes
2 shallots
½ bunch basil
3 stalks celery
Handful of fresh oregano
2 cloves garlic
1 tablespoon olive oil
Juice of ½ lemon
1 tablespoon local raw honey (or agave syrup)
Water to desired consistency

1. Place all ingredients into the blender and secure the lid. Be sure to start by putting the tomatoes in first.
2. Turn blender on and increase the speed to 10, then flip to switch to high speed.
3. Blend for 5 to 6 minutes or until hot.

This is a heart healthy way to eat "raw" tomato soup. With a low temperature thermometer keep the soup at 115 degrees or less. It is also gluten free, vegetarian, low cholesterol, and diabetic friendly.

Avocado Soup

2-3 cups of water (filtered or bottled is best)
2 avocados, peeled & pitted
21/2 tablespoons miso, brown or white
2 tablespoons olive oil
Juice of 1 lime

1 teaspoon fresh rosemary or herb of choice
½ teaspoon dried chipotle (optional)

1. Place all ingredients into the blender and secure the lid. Be sure to start by putting the water in first.
2. Turn blender on and increase the speed to 10, then flip to switch to high speed.
3. Blend for 5 to 6 minutes or until hot (115 degrees on low temperature thermometer).
4. Sprinkle diced tomatoes on top & serve.

This is a healthy way to eat at only 89 calories per 1 cup serving, it is also gluten free, vegetarian, low cholesterol, and diabetic friendly.

Chilled Cucumber Soup

Filtered or bottled water to desired consistency
1 organic cucumber
Large handful of fresh dill
½ cup sugar snap peas
2 cloves garlic
Chopped green onion to taste (1/2 cup)
5 scallions
1 organic lemon, peeled
1 tablespoon olive oil
1 tablespoon apple vinegar cider
1 tablespoon raw honey
Sea salt & freshly cracked black pepper, to taste

1. Place all ingredients into the blender and secure the lid. Be sure to start by putting the water in first.
2. Turn blender on and increase the speed to 10, then flip to switch to high speed.
3. Blend for 5 to 6 minutes or until hot.

Serve chilled & garnished with dill. This is a healthy way to eat your veggies. It is also gluten free, vegetarian, low cholesterol, and diabetic friendly.

Thai Soup

2 cups warm filtered or bottled water
3 carrots
1 orange bell pepper
¾ cup soaked cashews
¾ cup almond milk
1 tablespoon nama shoyu
1 tablespoon agave nectar
½ jalapeno pepper
Tablespoon cilantro
1 tablespoon curry powder
2 teaspoons sea salt
Fresh chives, chopped for garnish

1. Place all ingredients into the blender and secure the lid. Be sure to start by putting the water in first.

2. Turn blender on and increase the speed to 10, then flip to switch to high speed.
3. Blend for 5 to 6 minutes or until hot.

This is a heart healthy recipe. It is also gluten free, vegetarian, low cholesterol, and diabetic friendly.

Very Berry Soup

¼ cup water
$^{2}/_{3}$ cup milk
$^{1}/_{3}$ cup orange juice
4 cups fresh or frozen strawberries (thawed)
2 cups vanilla yogurt
6 tablespoons agave syrup
1 teaspoon fresh lemon juice
2 cups raspberries, fresh or frozen (almost thawed)

1. Place all ingredients except for half (3 tablespoons) of the agave syrup, lemon juice, and raspberries into the blender and secure the lid.
2. Turn blender on and increase to high speed for 30-60 seconds or until desired consistency is reached.
3. Pour soup base into bowls.
4. Place the remaining 3 tablespoons of agave syrup, lemon juice, and raspberries into the blender and secure the lid.

5. Blend for 20-30 seconds and drizzle over soup base.

This is not only a great dish for your eyes, it is also heart healthy, gluten free, and vegetarian. *Blendtec*

Batters and Syrups

"In general, mankind, since the improvement in cookery, eats twice as much as nature requires." ~Benjamin Franklin

Lowfat waffles

4 egg whites
2 cups skim milk
1 tablespoon unsweetened applesauce
1 cup oat bran
1 cup unbleached flour
1 ½ teaspoons baking powder
1 ½ teaspoons baking soda

1. Place egg whites, skim milk, and applesauce into the blender and secure the lid.
2. Turn blender on and increase the speed to 10, then flip to switch to high speed.
3. Blend for 30.
4. Reduce speed to 5.
5. Add oat bran, flour, baking powder, and baking soda. Replace lid.

6. Blend for 30 more seconds or until mixed.
7. Bake in waffle iron.

Makes approximately 8 waffles. Each waffle is only 115 calories, and they are also heart healthy, low fat, low cholesterol, and diabetic friendly. *Vitamix*

Whole Wheat Yogurt Pancakes

1 ¼ cups of water (filtered or bottled is best)
1 cup whole wheat flour
1 teaspoon baking soda
¾ cup plain yogurt
½ cup steel cut oats
1 cup blueberries (or other favorite fruit)

1. Place flour and baking soda into the blender and secure the lid.
2. Turn blender on and increase the speed to 10, then flip to switch to high speed.
3. Blend for 10 seconds or until mixed.
4. Reduce speed to 4.
5. Blend for 5 more seconds creating a hole in the flour mixture.
6. Stop blender and remove lid.
7. Add yogurt and water.
8. Turn on blender and increase speed to 6.

9. Blend for 15 seconds or until mixed. If necessary, stop and use spatula to loosen any flour from sides of container.

10. Reduce speed to 4 and add the steel cut oats.

11. Blend for 5 more seconds or until just mixed. Do not over mix. If batter is too thin you can add more oats to thicken.

12. Stir in fruit and cook.

These delicious whole wheat yogurt pancakes are only 152 calories per pancake, they are also heart healthy, low fat, low cholesterol, vegetarian and diabetic friendly. *Vitamix*

Pineapple Syrup

3 cups pineapple
¾ cup agave (or other natural sweetener to taste)
1 teaspoon lemon juice

1. Place all ingredients into the blender and secure the lid. Be sure to start by putting the water in first.

2. Turn blender on and increase to high speed.

3. Blend about 3 minutes.

This delicious syrup is only 67 calories per ¼ cup serving. It is also heart healthy, low fat, low cholesterol, vegetarian, and gluten free. *Vitamix*

Apricot Syrup

3 cups apricots
¾ cup agave (or other natural sweetener to taste)
1 teaspoon lemon juice

1. Place all ingredients into the blender and secure the lid. Be sure to start by putting the water in first.
2. Turn blender on and increase to high speed.
3. Blend about 3 minutes.

This delicious syrup is only 67 calories per ¼ cup serving. It is also heart healthy, low fat, low cholesterol, vegetarian, and gluten free. *Vitamix*

Banana Oat Pancakes

½ cup steel cut oats
½ cup unbleached flour (can use whole wheat or rice flour)
¼ cup soy flour
1 tablespoon baking powder
1 ½ cups plain soymilk
2 peeled bananas
1 teaspoon vanilla extract

1. Place all ingredients, except bananas, into the blender and secure the lid. Be sure to start by putting the soymilk in first.
2. Turn blender on and increase to high speed.
3. Blend for about 10-20 seconds.

4. Reduce speed to low and add the bananas. Blend for another 10-30 seconds to desired consistency.

These pancakes are only 80 calories each. They are also heart healthy, low fat, low cholesterol, vegetarian, and diabetic friendly. *Vitamix*

Purees

"If we're not willing to settle for junk living, we certainly shouldn't settle for junk food."

~Sally Edwards

Pear Baby Food

1 chopped, cored pear

1. Steam the chopped pear in small pan until tender.
2. Place steamed pear and ¼ cup of the cooking water into the blender and secure the lid.
3. Blend on low speed for 10-20 seconds for a chunky consistency.
4. Blend on medium high for 10-20 seconds for a smoother pureed consistency. You can adjust by adding water as needed

You can do this with most any fruit or vegetable with some slight modification. This is an incredible way to get your baby the full nutrients they need from the foods you feed them. *Vitamix*

Dan's Easy Sweet Potato Baby Food

1 medium to large sweet
½ chopped, cored pear

1. Steam the Sweet potato and chopped pear in small (separate) pans until tender.
2. Place steamed sweet potato and pear and ¼ cup of the cooking water into the blender and secure the lid.
3. Blend on low to medium speed for 10-20 seconds for a chunky consistency.
4. Blend on medium to high for 10-20 seconds for a smoother pureed consistency. You can adjust by adding water as needed

You can do this with most any fruit or vegetable with some slight modification. This is an incredible way to get your baby the full nutrients they need from the foods you feed them. *Vitamix*

Pureed Bananas

2 ripe peeled bananas, halved

1. Place ingredients into the blender and secure the lid.

2. Turn blender on and increase to medium speed.
3. Blend for 5-10 seconds or until desired consistency is reached.

This going green smoothie is only 42 calories per 2 tablespoon serving, it is also heart healthy, low fat, low carb, low cholesterol, vegetarian, gluten free, and diabetic friendly. *Vitamix*

Pureed Carrots

2 cups fresh steamed carrots (cut into 1 in. pieces)
3 tablespoons water

1. Place all ingredients into the blender and secure the lid.
2. Turn blender on and increase to medium speed.
3. Blend for 30-45 seconds or until desired consistency is reached.

This going green smoothie is only 9 calories per 2 tablespoon serving, it is also heart healthy, low fat, low carb, low cholesterol, vegetarian, gluten free, and diabetic friendly. *Vitamix*

Pureed Corn

1 cup steamed corn

¼ cup water

1. Place ingredients into the blender and secure the lid.
2. Turn blender on and increase to medium speed.
3. Blend for 5-10 seconds or until desired consistency is reached.

This going green smoothie is only 22 calories per 2 tablespoon serving, it is also heart healthy, low fat, low carb, low cholesterol, vegetarian, gluten free, and diabetic friendly. *Vitamix*

Pureed Green Beans

2 cups steamed fresh green beans
2 tablespoons water

1. Place ingredients into the blender and secure the lid.
2. Turn blender on and increase to medium speed.
3. Blend for 5-10 seconds or until desired consistency is reached.

You may need to stop blender to scrap down ingredients to make sure everything is pureed evenly.

This going green smoothie is only 6 calories per 2 tablespoon serving, it is also heart healthy, low fat, low carbs, low cholesterol, vegetarian, gluten free, and diabetic friendly. *Vitamix*

Pureed Peaches

2 cups fresh or frozen peeled peaches

1. Place ingredients into the blender and secure the lid.
2. Turn blender on and increase to medium speed.
3. Blend for 5-10 seconds or until desired consistency is reached.

This going green smoothie is only 12 calories per 2 tablespoon serving, it is also heart healthy, low fat, low carbs, low cholesterol, vegetarian, gluten free, and diabetic friendly. *Vitamix*

Pureed Peas

2 cups steamed fresh peas
2 tablespoons water

1. Place ingredients into the blender and secure the lid.
2. Turn blender on and increase to medium speed.
3. Blend for 5-10 seconds or until desired consistency is reached.

You may need to stop blender to scrap down ingredients to make sure everything is pureed evenly.

This going green smoothie is only 14 calories per 2 tablespoon serving, it is also heart healthy, low fat, low carbs, low cholesterol, vegetarian, gluten free, and diabetic friendly. *Vitamix*

Pureed Squash

2 cups squash, cooked and removed from peel
¼ cup of the cooking water

1. Place all ingredients into the blender and secure the lid.
2. Turn blender on and increase to medium speed.
3. Blend for 5-10 seconds or until desired consistency is reached.

You may need to stop blender to scrap down ingredients to make sure everything is pureed evenly.

This going green smoothie is only 4 calories per 2 tablespoon serving, it is also heart healthy, low fat, low carbs, low cholesterol, vegetarian, gluten free, and diabetic friendly. *Vitamix*

Smoky Pepper Puree

1 cup red peppers
2 tablespoons extra-virgin olive oil
1 to 2 chipotle pepper, seeded (you can substitute green peppers and add ½ to 1 tablespoon of chipotle powder)
2 garlic cloves

1. Place all ingredients into the blender and secure the lid. Be sure to start by putting the water in first.
2. Turn blender on and increase to high speed.
3. Blend only until pureed. You do not want to liquefy. Add salt to taste.

This is a great topping for chicken or steak. This puree is also heart healthy, low fat, and low cholesterol.

Pureed Chicken

1 cup boneless, skinless chicken breast, cooked and cut into cubes
⅓ cup of the cooking water

1. Place all ingredients into the blender and secure the lid.
2. Turn blender on and increase to medium speed.
3. Blend for 30-45 seconds or until desired consistency is reached.

You may need to stop blender to scrap down ingredients to make sure everything is pureed evenly.

This going green smoothie is only 18 calories per 2 tablespoon serving, it is also heart healthy, low fat, low carbs, low cholesterol, vegetarian, gluten free, and diabetic friendly. *Vitamix*

Delightful Desserts

"Did you ever stop to taste a carrot? Not just eat it, but taste it? You can't taste the beauty and energy of the earth in a Twinkie." ~Astrid Alauda

Very Berry Fruit Ice

1 cup frozen strawberries
1 cup frozen blueberries
1 cup frozen raspberries (you can also use boysenberries or blackberries
1 cup cold water
4 to 6 ice cubes
(Optional - agave syrup to taste)
(Optional – 1 teaspoon fresh mint)

1. Place all ingredients into the blender and secure the lid. Be sure to start by putting the water in first.
2. Turn blender on and increase to high speed.
3. Blend only until mixed. Over blending here will only warm and melt contents.

You can also put this delicious dessert in the freezer to firm up if needed. This dessert is also heart healthy, low fat, low cholesterol, and diabetic friendly. *Magic Bullet*

Apple Pie Ice Cream

1 6 oz. can frozen apple juice concentrate
2 tablespoons lowfat vanilla yogurt
1/3 cup powdered milk
1/2 apple, quartered
1 tablespoon vanilla extract
1/4 teaspoon cinnamon
1 ripe banana (optional)
3 cups ice cubes

1. Place all ingredients into the blender and secure the lid. Be sure to start by putting the apple juice and liquids in first.
2. Turn blender on and increase to high speed.
3. Blend only 30-60 seconds, the sound of the motor will change and four mounds should form in the mixture. Stop machine. Do not overmix or melting will occur. Serve immediately.

If the mixture has more of a milkshake consistency you can firm it up by adding another cup of ice cubes. Again, only blend until smooth. This dessert is also heart healthy, low fat, low cholesterol, and diabetic friendly. *Vitamix*

Banana Ice Cream

3 peeled bananas
2 tablespoons agave syrup (or other natural sweetener)
1 cup skim, 1% or 2% milk
3 cups ice cubes

1. Place all ingredients into the blender and secure the lid. Be sure to start by putting the milk in first.
2. Turn blender on and increase to high speed.
3. Blend only 30-60 seconds, the sound of the motor will change and four mounds should form in the mixture. Stop machine. Do not over mix or melting will occur. Serve immediately.

If the mixture has more of a milkshake consistency you can firm it up by adding another cup of ice cubes. Again, only blend until smooth. This dessert is also heart healthy, low fat, low cholesterol, and diabetic friendly. *Vitamix*

Strawberry Cheesecake Ice Cream

1 cup nonfat half and half
1 cup reduced fat sour cream
6 oz. low fat cream cheese
½ teaspoon vanilla extract
2 tablespoons fresh lemon juice
¾ cup agave syrup (or other natural sweetener)

3 cups frozen strawberries
1 cups ice cubes
Low fat whipped topping (optional)
Fresh blueberries (optional)

1. Place all ingredients into the blender and secure the lid. Be sure to start by putting the milk in first.
2. Turn blender on and increase to high speed. Use tamper to safely press ingredients into the blades.
3. Blend only 30-60 seconds, the sound of the motor will change and four mounds should form in the mixture. Stop machine. Do not over mix or melting will occur. Serve immediately.

If the mixture has more of a milkshake consistency you can firm it up by adding another cup of ice cubes. Again, only blend until smooth.

Researchers have done studies showing that blueberries help improve two age related concerns: loss of memory and loss of coordination. This dessert is also heart healthy, low fat, low cholesterol, and diabetic friendly. *Vitamix*

French Vanilla Shake

1 cup vanilla nonfat frozen yogurt (lowfat Ice cream can also be used)
¼ teaspoon vanilla extract
½ cup skim milk
1 cups ice cubes

1. Place all ingredients into the blender and secure the lid. Be sure to start by putting the milk in first.
2. Turn blender on and increase to high speed.
3. Blend only 45-60 seconds or until desired consistency is reached. Serve immediately.

For a French Vanilla Malt, add 2 tablespoons of malted milk powder.

For a non-dairy alternative you can use Soy milk and Soy ice cream.

This dessert is also heart healthy, low fat, low cholesterol, and diabetic friendly. *Vitamix*

Creamy Spiced Cider

3 ½ cups apple cider
1 large, quartered apple
1 large peeled orange
2 ½ cups frozen nonfat vanilla yogurt
1 teaspoon cinnamon
1 teaspoon nutmeg

1. Place all ingredients into the blender and secure the lid. Be sure to start by putting the milk in first.
2. Turn blender on and increase to high speed.
3. Blend only 30-45 seconds or until desired consistency is reached. Serve immediately.

At only 196 calories per 1 cup serving, this dessert is also heart healthy, low fat, low cholesterol, and diabetic friendly. *Vitamix*

Heart Smart Chocolate Fondue

1 cup plain or vanilla soy milk, heated to simmer
12 oz. semi-sweet dark chocolate (broken into pieces)
1 tablespoon butter
¼ cup cream sherry (optional)

1. Place all ingredients into the blender and secure the lid. Be sure to start by putting the milk in first.
2. Turn blender on and increase to high speed.
3. Blend 2 to 3 minutes or until melted and smooth. If using sherry, add just before turning off and blend for 5 more seconds. Pour into fondue pot and enjoy.

Some great dippers include – sponge cake, pound cake, apple slices, pear slices, marshmallows, strawberries, bananas, and pineapple chunks. This great tasting fondue is also vegetarian, low carb, low cholesterol, and gluten free. *Vitamix*

Guilt Free Whipped Topping

1 cup cold skim milk
1 ½ tablespoons agave (or another natural sweetener)
1 teaspoon vanilla extract
1 teaspoon xanthan gum

1. Place all ingredients into the blender and secure the lid. Be sure to start by putting the milk in first.
2. Turn blender on and increase to medium speed.
3. Blend only 10-15 seconds – add the xanthan gum and blend for 15-30 more seconds or until mixture forms four mounds. Serve within 2 hours.

You can substitute other natural flavored extracts for the vanilla. At only 11 calories per 2 tablespoon serving, this dessert topping is also heart healthy, low fat, low cholesterol, and gluten free. *Vitamix*

Honeydew Sorbet

1 cup melon liqueur
1 pound diced frozen honeydew melon
½ cup ice cubes

1. Place all ingredients into the blender in the order listed and secure the lid.
2. Turn blender on and increase to high speed. Use the tamper to press down the ingredients.

3. Blend only 30-60 seconds, the sound of the motor will change and four mounds should form in the mixture. Stop machine. Do not over mix or melting will occur. Serve immediately.

If consistency is not thick enough you can put into an airtight container and place in the freezer for 1 to 3 hours before serving. Only 137 calories per ½ cup serving, this dessert is also heart healthy, low fat, low cholesterol, and vegetarian. *Vitamix*

Pumpkin Bars

1 cup canola oil
1 ⅔ cups agave (or other natural sweetener to taste)
4 eggs
15.5 oz. can pumpkin
1 ½ cups unbleached flour
½ cup soy flour
1 teaspoon cinnamon
1 teaspoon salt
1 teaspoon baking soda
2 teaspoons baking powder

1. Preheat oven to 350F. spray 10x15x1 inch pan with cooking spray.
2. Place the sugar, oil eggs and pumpkin into the blender and secure the lid.
3. Turn blender on and increase to medium speed.
4. Blend about 15-30 seconds until smooth.

5. Combine the flour and spices in a separate bowl and then, with blender off, add to the mixture in the blender.

6. Turn blender on and increase to high speed

7. Blend 30-45 seconds.

8. Pour batter into pan and bake for 25-30 minutes or until a toothpick comes out clean.

This makes 15 bars per batch and at only 297 calories each they make a great between meal snack. They are also heart healthy and vegetarian.
Vitamix

Food For Thought

Our bodies require vitamins and minerals, also know as nutrients, to support life. We get those nutrients from the foods that we eat. This includes drinking half your body weight in ounces of water ever day.

"If we're not willing to settle for junk living, we certainly shouldn't settle for junk food." ~Sally Edwards

Does it make more sense to eat foods that are grown with pesticides and chemicals and steroids to make them bigger faster?

"We are living in a world today where lemonade is made from artificial flavors and furniture polish is made from real lemons." ~Alfred E. Newman

"There are 70 pesticides that are listed as known or probable carcinogens, based on animal testing. Of those 70, 44 are in use today, and 23 are used on our food."
~ Gina Solomon, specialist in internal medicine [2001]

Why not eat foods that are grown the way they are meant to grow? Scientific studies have show that naturally grown, organic fruits and vegetables have more of the nutrients we need.

"When you look at an apple, some people would say the non-organic apple is cheaper than the organic apple. But when you factor in what you're receiving in terms of vitamins, minerals, etc., the organic apple - on that basis - is cheaper than the non-organic apple."
~ Jerry Kay, on Beyond Organic

"When you go to the grocery store, you find that the cheapest calories are the ones that are going to make you the fattest - the added sugars and fats in processed foods."
~ Michael Pollan, author of The Omnivore's Dilemma

Many people have said things like this:
"Don't eat anything your great-great grandmother wouldn't recognize as food. There are a great many food-like items in the supermarket your ancestors wouldn't recognize as food (Go-Gurt? Breakfast-cereal bars? Nondairy creamer?); stay away from these." -Michael Pollan

"If you think humans are meat-eaters then try eating the animal raw like every other meat-eater on the planet. If something is not palatable in its raw state then you probably shouldn't be eating it."
~ David Wolfe, author, Nature's First Law: The Raw-Food Diet

Finally, here are some great quotes and some facts that you may not have known.
"Now that I've got kids, it's become really important for me on the health front to try to buy as much organic produce as possible."
~ Jamie Oliver, UK celebrity chef, in BBC Good Food magazine

"If the diet is wrong, then medicines are of no use. If diet is right, then the medicines are of no need"
~ Ayurveda Scripture 500 BC

"It's bizarre that the produce manager is more important to my children's health than the pediatrician." ~Meryl Streep

"Plant a radish, get a radish, never any doubt. That's why I love vegetables, you know what they're about!" ~Tom Jones and Harvey Schmidt

"Unlike your genetics, you do have a choice over what foods you eat and their subsequent impact on your well-being."
~ Mitch Thrower

"Yesterday I saw a child wearing a T-shirt that said, "If you love me, don't feed me junk food." I was delighted to see this, but I also know how difficult it can be to feed our children well, particularly when the foods that are most convenient and the most heavily advertised are often the ones we should avoid. Joel Fuhrman's new book is a blessing, because it makes it so much easier. It is excellent, and full of clarity, wisdom, and guidance you can trust. It can indeed give you the power to shape your child's health destiny - John Robbins"
~ Joel Fuhrman

"Eating a vegetarian diet, walking (exercising) everyday, and meditating is considered radical. Allowing someone to slice your chest open and graft your leg veins in your heart is considered normal and conservative."
~ Dean Ornish

The saddest and scariest quote of them all is:

"Amount spent annually by McDonald's advertising its products: $800 million - Amount spent annually by the National Cancer Institute promoting fruits and vegetables: $1 million."
~ John Robbins

We all have to do our part to make this better. For your health, buy organic when ever possible!

Always ask yourself…
When is Now a Good Time?

Create A Great Day!

“How am I going to live today
in order to create the tomorrow
I'm committed to?”

~ Tony Robbins

Made in the USA
San Bernardino, CA
26 December 2012